D0041327

Cosmic Botany

A GUIDE TO CRYSTAL AND PLANT SOUL MATES
FOR PEACE, HAPPINESS, AND ABUNDANCE

TANYA LICHTENSTEIN

A TarcherPerigee Book

tarcherperigee
an imprint of Penguin Random House LLC
penguinrandomhouse.com

Copyright © 2020 by Tanya Lichtenstein
Penguin supports copyright. Copyright fuels creativity, encourages diverse voices, promotes free speech, and creates a vibrant culture. Thank you for buying an authorized edition of this book and for complying with copyright laws by not reproducing, scanning, or distributing any part of it in any form without permission. You are supporting writers and allowing Penguin to continue to publish books for every reader.

Most Tarcher/Penguin books are available at special quantity discounts for bulk purchase for sales promotions, premiums, fund-raising, and educational needs. Special books or book excerpts also can be created to fit specific needs. For details, write: SpecialMarkets@penguinrandomhouse.com.

Library of Congress Cataloging-in-Publication Data
Names: Lichtenstein, Tanya, author.
Title: Cosmic botany: a guide to crystal and plant soul mates for peace, happiness, and abundance / Tanya Lichtenstein.
Description: [New York] : TarcherPerigee, an imprint of Penguin Random House LLC, [2020] | Includes index.
Identifiers: LCCN 2019038447 (print) | LCCN 2019038448 (ebook) | ISBN 9780593084205 (hardcover) | ISBN 9780593084212 (epub)
Subjects: LCSH: Plants—Therapeutic use. | Crystals—Therapeutic use. | Healing. | Energy medicine.
Classification: LCC RZ401 .L58 2020 (print) | LCC RZ401 (ebook) | DDC 615.8/528—dc23
LC record available at https://lccn.loc.gov/2019038447
LC ebook record available at https://lccn.loc.gov/2019038448

Printed in China
1 3 5 7 9 10 8 6 4 2

Book design by Laura K. Corless
Interior art: watercolor texture © Lena Bukovsky / Shutterstock.com

For my babies

CHAPTER TWO
You've Got This

CHAPTER THREE
No Bad Days

CHAPTER FOUR
The Plant & Crystal Diet

INTRODUCTION

A house is not a home without plants . . . or crystals.

Who doesn't love plants? Gorgeous, overflowing greenery is covering blogs, magazines, and our favorite Instagram accounts. Interior design is going wild—literally! The trend is so strong, even a plant novice may be considering adopting a succulent or two. Green thumb or not, chances are you're already cohabiting with some of these beauties. Plants are great: they add fresh energy to your home and even clean the very air you breathe by filtering out pollutants like dust, pollen, and dirt through their leaves and roots. Plants are extraordinary; no wonder we love them so much.

Crystals are having a sparkly moment, too. They bring us high-vibrational energies and add beauty to our lives. In fact, you may have a favorite crystal tucked in your bra right now, you rock goddess. Crystals are everlasting mineral blends that carry sage wisdom in their shiny facets.

And when you fill your home with *both*, you can experience what happens when you pair them together; it's nothing less than modern magic. I learned this myself when I decorated a planter with crystals and noticed that the plant was more vibrant. Plants and crystals are soul mates. It's a timeless love story that spans back to the origins of the cosmos, plants and crystals working in perfect harmony. The crystal nourishes the plant with supercharged vibes to encourage growth and well-being, and the plant recharges the crystal with grounded energy from the earth.

Crystals work with a constant flow of high-vibrational energy in their varied structures (faceted crystals, tumbled stones, raw clusters, etc.) and they need recharging. You may have heard of using water, sunlight, or sage, but a plant is also a great tool. Plants have the ability to transform negative energy into positive energy, much in the same way they filter the air. Like tiny ecosystems of good vibrations, plants and crystals continuously renew and recharge each other's energy. It's cosmic teamwork.

Plants' and crystals' colors and textures make any home refined and beautiful, but this book is about so much more than decorating with lovely plants and pretty gems. It's about alchemy and the special energy that occurs when they are matched in complementary ways. That's why I'm excited to share this guide of well-chosen crystal and plant combinations, along with the wondrous vibes they create. Whether you're craving a deep sense of serenity, need motivation in your life, or you want to align with your higher purpose, you'll find the perfect combo here.

I hope this book inspires you to fill your home with plants and crystals that will bring you peace, happiness, and abundance. There are infinite combinations to enjoy. It's a pleasure to mix the two and to experience the supercharged energy they bring into your world. The important thing is to have fun with your design and lead with your heart.

Just think, you are a talented matchmaker and you don't even know it yet. All you have to do is start.

TANYA

CHAPTER ONE

Fractals of Love

You Are Stardust

Few things bring us joy like a rough chunk of amethyst. They're the crystal equivalent of brownies—everyone wants one. Raw amethyst clusters are most popular and vary from deep mulberry hues to the palest of lavender. This gem is a perennial hit for its beauty and extraordinary traits. It is an ideal stone for beginners, too.

Did you know that amethysts reduce anxiety and help you connect to your intuition? The reason: amethyst resonates strongly with the air element, so it has a cool, reassuring energy that will support you when you need a boost. In fact, every crystal holds a balance of the four elements (earth, air, fire, and water) in its facets, and often exhibits one of them prominently. Breezy amethyst has cool and collected energy that you can rely on when needed.

A super boho and nomadic perennial, air plants don't need soil to grow in and thus are not limited to planters like common houseplants. Air plants are free and thrive in many environments because they are epiphytes, and make their home in soaring tree lines in the wild. They require little care because they pull moisture from the air for nourishment. These beauties are wild and flourish in unusual circumstances. Most resemble sage-green pasta bundles, but some are likely to be mistaken for plants from another galaxy.

THE VIBE

When you're feeling sad and your self-esteem is a little less than stellar, look up at the stars and appreciate our elegant universe. It's astonishing to think that the very minerals found in stars are also found in you. You are stardust! Amethyst helps you connect to these higher realms with ease and gently dissolves any barriers holding you back from remembering this truth. Your awesomeness is untamed and without limitation. Hey, if air plants can defy what's normal and still thrive, then so can you. Believe in yourself. Your true nature is brilliant, expansive, and beautiful—just like the stars themselves.

Spirit Junkie

If there were a high crystal council for ranking the best crystals, then spirit quartz would be number one. Spirit quartz became popular in 2001, like most millennials. In fact, it's the quintessential millennial stone—sparkly, special, and full of wisdom beyond its years. Glittering faceted clusters that look like star particles surround terminated crystal formations to give it big cosmic energy. Each one is unique due to a gradient effect that produces a tonal range of purple, pink, peach, and white. Spirit quartz has a celestial heritage and its clusters hold ancient archives of universal knowledge. Being in the presence of one will put you into the spiritual flow and help you connect with the part of you that's pure, loving, full of knowing, and understands that you are one with the universe.

You may be drawn to watermelon begonia if you long for a deeper connection to all things because it pulls you in with celestial, earthy energy. Watermelon begonias have dewdrop-shaped leaves with variegated patterns that look like galaxies swirling into existence. Their dark green spirals begin at a central point and expand across the rounded leaves in perfect symmetry, giving off an energy of harmony, balance, and endless renewal. The wisdom of this design is echoed throughout all of nature and the universe. It's amazing when you find these kinds of natural elements that reflect an entire macrocosm in their patterning.

THE VIBE

When you expand your spiritual awareness beyond the world around you, you start to feel connected to the entire universe and you elevate your daily experiences. Living in this state of wonder raises your vibration and makes you happier. Spirit quartz and watermelon begonia remind you to focus on your inner growth and guide you with loving energy. Watermelon begonia helps you recognize that there's a sacred intelligence behind everything, and that there's more to life than what you can see. When you're ready to learn more, spirit quartz will help you understand energy, vibration, and how your thoughts and feelings shape your experiences. You will begin to look at your life in a different way, see the beauty and connectedness of everything, and take comfort in the fact that you are part of something greater and will always be guided.

Sparkly Jumpsuit Goddess

Most crystals are cooling (think aquamarine, amethyst, and moonstone), but some are warming, like citrine, sunstone, and carnelian. In general, warming crystals differ from the cooler varieties in that they have fiery, activating energy. If you're drawn to carnelians, it's because they have a spicy, sensual energy like the scent of tuberose. You may also crave carnelian if you love juicy shades of guava, desert landscapes, or the deep red-orange glow of a sunset. Warm orange tones have a feminine, life-affirming vitality that makes life richer. Carnelians carry this energy beautifully, in the form of soft, polished stones that balance wild passion with grounded life-force.

Pink princess philodendron has storybook variegations on its glossy leaves. The heart-shaped foliage tells stories of love, courage, and self-expression in contrasting pink and green tones. It's a precious-looking plant with a fierce energy that will help you access your heart-centered courage to express your emotions. Pink princess philodendron asks you to embrace your true feelings because your emotional nature is part of what makes you a rare, loving soul.

THE VIBE

You're just waiting to embrace your divine feminine nature. It's nurturing, sensual, bold, creative, and free. When you acknowledge that these aspects are part of your being, you can step into your role as a modern goddess, and then buy her a sparkly jumpsuit (because she prefers them over caftans). Pink princess philodendron and carnelian hold this sacred feminine energy with a boldness that shows in their natural beauty, and they will inspire you to step into your power. Like a carnelian, you can make everything glow; that's the raw power of the divine feminine. Pink princess philodendron gives you the courage to honor this aspect of yourself without hesitation. Your true nature is untamed, like the wild plants and crystals you so admire. Let their energy inspire you to be the same. Trust your inner goddess and follow your intrinsic feminine wisdom.

Hello, Sunshine

Pink halite is a tough-looking crystal that's actually quite fragile, a plait of salt crystals stacked neatly together that look like melted pastel marshmallows. Pink halite has yummy energy! Though delicate because it's made of salt, the smart lattice structure allows each layer to support the next one. Hard and soft is the energy of this heart-centered crystal. It has the strength to clear emotional hardships and a nurturing vibe to help you heal. The salt purifies negativity and dissolves it into neutrality. It's a good reminder that salty tears are just a release of sadness so you are free to connect with love again.

Peace lilies' tranquil vibe will brighten any space. A paper-thin spathe flower with the graceful carriage of a ballerina balances above a thick blanket of dark green, glossy leaves. Peace lilies have an understated elegance and each may produce only a handful of blooms, maintaining a harmonious look. A symbol of peace, the plant's spathe has a gentle curved shape that wraps you up like a warm, uplifting hug.

THE VIBE

If you're ready to clear tough feelings like sadness, grief, and anger, an emotional edit may be in order. Pink halite and peace lily are the perfect helpers to support your emotional body through this process. Peace lily surrounds you with loving energy so you can mend in a safe space, in your own time. Healing happens in layers and cannot be rushed. When you're fully anchored in its calming spirit, settle into your body and get in touch with your tough emotions. Where do you feel them in your body? You may feel emotions trapped in your heart-space or back. Let pink halite's saltiness dissolve those emotional blockages. The crystal will give you the support you need to release this energy by whatever means feel best. You might feel like crying, or maybe a nap is in order. Be gentle with yourself. Healing old wounds can be an exquisite experience when you have the support of the right plant and crystal.

Bloom Where You Are

You never forget your first rose quartz. The stone just wants to nurture. When you connect to this rosy energy, you feel supported, loved, and hopeful. Other crystals have an intensity that can feel overwhelming, so you're more of a match for a rose quartz if you crave peace and comfort. Rose quartz crystals invite you to *be*. There's nothing to do, nothing that needs your attention; just sit and imagine loving pink energy all around you. Soon, you'll realize that love is the language you need to bring to every moment. This simple crystal may be teaching you the greatest lesson of all.

When you find heart-shaped leaves, it's a wink from nature that says, "I love you and I've got your back." How adorable is that? Sweetheart hoyas are succulent lovebugs that start out as a single leaf and have the potential to grow more buds. The plant evolves slowly, often taking a few years to fully bloom. For a long stretch of time, that single leaf will sit in a decorative planter, just waiting for its moment. The potential for expansion is always there, even though outer appearances may not indicate so. Sweetheart hoya teaches you to be content in the still moments, even if you're frustrated with your cir-

cumstances. Remember, you're always moving toward your highest potential, so never mark your progress by comparing yourself to others. Observe how a single heart-shaped leaf has the energy to bloom into a collection of green hearts with time and patience.

THE VIBE

Be patient while you're becoming the best version of you. Every day you're learning and growing. Your life may look the same, but those quiet moments of introspection are creating small changes within. Sometimes these developments cannot be seen, but they will be measured as a lifetime of accumulated wisdom. Sweetheart hoya shows you how to make yourself at home in the present moment. It's a plant that holds the possibility of expanding beyond its current surroundings under favorable conditions, and the same is true of you. What would happen if you had more empathy for yourself? That's exactly what rose quartz will teach you. When you are surrounded by love, it makes your journey feel like less of an odyssey. Discouragement and other negative emotions about not being where you want to be are handled with compassion. Nothing blooms under duress, and a little encouragement and love is what you needed all along. You are in the process of becoming the best bloom you can be.

Cosmic Soul Mates

You can't buy love, but at least you can buy tangerine quartz. Its terminated points are filled with passion and citrus-crush colors, and if you want to reinvigorate your love life or heal romantic wounds, this is your wingman. The crystal's warm energy will put your heart at ease so you can find the love you long for. It's like energetic vitamin C for romance. It's OK to supplement vitamins for your health, so why wouldn't you supplement crystals to improve your love life?

You can only see so many anthuriums before you develop a serious plant-crush. Their beauty is unstructured and not like typical flowers. Instead, their waxy flowers bloom in ultra-flattering lip gloss shades. Anthuriums are cool-girl plants that live up to the hype. Owning one will make you feel like you live in a fancy showroom that gives out trendy skin-care samples. Beauty aside, they're symbols of love and abundance. When not in showrooms or appearing in lavish handbag campaigns, you can find them in the wild growing on other plants. They are epiphytes, which is a technical plant term meaning "they like to cuddle." Anthuriums are all about affection and attention, and it's time to take notice.

THE VIBE

Finding your soul mate is easier than you think and it requires much less labeling than a well-organized pantry. So why settle for the pantry of your dreams when you could have the partner of your dreams? In reality, you can have both, but let's focus on the soul mate part first. To find boundless love, you have to create loving energy in your home. Anthurium and tangerine quartz are the perfect bonded pair, a visual love letter, and they will help you set the backdrop for an epic love story. Use tangerine quartz to remove blockages from past heartbreaks and flood your heart with a renewed passion. Anthurium will help you find your flirty side and draw love to you like a magnet. A deep connection with someone is possible. Just imagine, you could be building the pantry of your dreams with a soul mate by your side!

Cosmic tip: An anthurium with two blooms will attract love faster, as a balanced pair creates romantic synergy.

Like Busy & Michelle

Lapis lazuli is valued for its dark-wash denim color. Rare lapis is solid blue, but stones with a mixture of blue, white, and golden pyrite are more popular. You may be attracted to lapis if you want to speak your truth and deepen your friendships. Both the color and the stone itself are potent symbols of loyalty, giving meaning to the phrase "true blue friend."

Variegated rubber plant is *the* trendy plant of the moment. When you finally find one with the perfect pattern that makes your heart soar, you must show it off (#variegatedrubberplant). It's an easygoing plant that's also super tough because of its rubbery leaves and sap, and capable of growing to eight feet tall. Its full, spherical leaves are a symbol of abundance and good fortune.

THE VIBE

Life is better with plants, crystals, and best friends. A best friend is an extraordinary type of soul mate who cares for you unconditionally and will always help you find the best selfie light. That special bond has both deep roots and practical applications. Plus, only your bestie knows not to hug you too hard because of the aquamarine crystal you keep tucked in your bra for heart expansion (see? practical!). Busy and Michelle epitomize this type of soulful friendship. Are you ready to raise your vibration to the status of these super besties? The special energies of variegated rubber plant and lapis lazuli boost existing friendships and help create new ones.

The sturdiness of a rubber plant will reinforce any relationship until it's an immutable bond that can withstand ups and downs and long distances. Its rounded leaves increase good fortune and encourage your friendship to grow to new heights. Lapis lazuli increases loyalty, harmony, and clear communication. Its deep blue color represents the meaningful moments, while the golden flecks highlight the joy that's sprinkled throughout your friendship. Add these natural elements to your space and a treasured friendship will be eternally supported.

Soul Happy

Mojave turquoise is a mosaic of natural turquoise fragments, fused together with golden metals. Unifying copper keeps all of the colors in balance, giving the stone a terrazzo-like quality that vibrates with sublime energy. You get the same benefits of turquoise, but with a significant upgrade. Bold and bright, the gemstone helps with feelings of indifference and sadness. Buying one is a bit of a splurge over natural turquoise, but if it makes you happy (and it will), go for it.

Ornamental pampas grass is a wild-growing pom-pom that loves sunlight and dancing in the breeze, and is just happy to be here. Pampas grass grows in those places where bohemians go to find their muses—the coast and the desert—and that rugged, carefree energy abounds. Because this feathery stunner can be dried and preserved with a little nontoxic hair spray, it makes a beautiful and low-maintenance addition to your home. Sometimes green plants will overpower a space when neutrals would work best, and this is where pampas grass really sparkles, filling your home with sandy colors and airy energy, instead of bold color. It's the perfect no-stress, big-impact plant.

THE VIBE

Peace, joy, love, comfort, and gratitude are just a few emotions that work in a delicate balance to create happiness. When one is missing, that contentment is elusive. It takes some work to maintain a base level of happiness, so why not surround yourself with good vibes to make life a little easier? Pampas grass is laid-back and cheerful anywhere. Even the way it gracefully sways in the wind is a lesson, teaching you to go with the flow, instead of fighting the current and ending up broken. It's always best to stay in a high vibration no matter what kind of life circumstances are jostling you about. Likewise, Mojave turquoise holds space for many positive emotions in its patchwork structure. The entire gemstone is a living metaphor for happiness. The beauty and energy of the whole is dependent on individual facets (that is, emotions). Working with pampas grass and Mojave turquoise will have you feeling so upbeat that spontaneous hugging may occur. When you feel this happy, share your joy with the world.

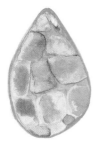

Memory Edit

Crystals hold memories far more ancient than your own and they are seasoned pros at helping with memory recall. A malachite heart is a great tool if you desire a harmonious connection between your heart and your mind. Deep green, marbled swirls in various shades pattern malachite like the rings of a tree stump, recording the passage of time. The glossy, finely polished surface of the stone reflects natural light. The spirit of malachite is protective and nurturing, and the balance of

reflective light with deep tones is what makes the stone so good at connecting your past memories to heartfelt emotions.

A canopy of leaves flooded with watercolor variegation adorns Krimson Princess Hoya with sweet energy. Once you discover that the plant produces aromatic flowers that smell faintly of chocolate, you will love this hoya even more! Charming leaf patterns, each one unique, are like special memories to cherish. Some make you blush, others make you smile, and the best ones knock you over with laughter. When paired with malachite, they create the foundation for lifelong happiness and warmth you feel in your heart.

THE VIBE

Happy memories create strong roots that you can draw from at any time to feel peace or bliss in the present moment. Memories are so much more than wistful remembrances. The energy and emotions associated with them shape who you are and deepen your wisdom. Life is a collection of recollections held in your heart and mind with affection, and accessing the past is a way to bring levity to the surface now. Everyone needs a joyful pick-me-up now and again, so why not use beautiful plants and crystals to revive the connection to your fondest memories? Malachite and Krimson Princess Hoya are natural archivists to assist you if your memories have been eroded by time. Krimson Princess Hoya will help you recall your extraordinary moments and appreciate the fact that each happy memory is like a beautiful leaf you can admire at any time. Hold malachite in your hand or against your heart to encode the stone with the energy of your most treasured moments from the past. Now, each time you look at the gem (or hold it near), you will connect the feeling of that memory to your heart. Joy abounds when you bring your happy past into the present!

No-Plan Weekend

If you want a crystal with soft energy and you're not vibing with pink rose quartz or purple amethyst, give lavender quartz a try. Lavender shades are rarely found in crystals, so when you find one, you know you have a truly exceptional stone. Lavender quartz's laid-back, nurturing, and serene energy will safeguard you from stress and life's ups and downs. It's here to remind you to relax and take a break because you're a human BEing, not a human DOing.

Goddesses of the forest, maidenhair ferns have feathery foliage with leaflet fractals. They look like celadon wisteria blooms and project a feminine energy that encourages you to go with the flow. Maidenhair ferns prefer a bath over sunbathing; this low-key plant longs for the tranquil space of a humid bathroom over the spotlight of a living room and creates a tiny canopy of peace wherever you place them. They know that a good steam will keep both of you hydrated and lush.

THE VIBE

This weekend, your only plan should be to have no plans. Whatever time you have is for downtime. Get busy going with the flow and doing what makes your heart soar. When you say "no" to planning, you leave room for connecting to your heart-space and doing what makes you happy. Maidenhair fern's love of simplicity inspires you to just chill out, and lavender quartz gives you the space to take a respite without guilt or stress. That supportive energy encourages you to slow down and discover what would make you glow in the moment. If that means putting all errands on hold and trying out the new brunch place in your 'hood, then so be it! Not all plants and crystals have activating energy, and lavender quartz and maidenhair fern bolster you if you feel like doing absolutely nothing. Sometimes resting is exactly what you need.

Worry Detox

Soapy blue-green amazonite is strongly aligned with water. It will help you wash away worries with its calming, neutralizing aura. Simply holding an amazonite in your hand supports proper energetic hygiene and calls in a sense of peace. Since tension and stress are low-vibrating states, they cannot exist in amazonite's presence. As you grow more accustomed to the stone, you'll notice yourself becoming more placid, too, and able to neutralize stress before it turns into a worry spiral.

The string-of-pearls plant has been brightening up shelfies for many years now. Its swoops of round leafy orbs drape over their planters with an exuberance that cannot be contained. You might be tempted to pop the spherical buds like bubble wrap, but please refrain; the succulent stores water in those pearly stems. String-of-pearls has a carefree energy and takes it all easy, and all those water-laden leaves hold the kinetic potential of a waterfall.

THE VIBE

A waterfall is in constant motion, cleansing everything it crashes over. That's why it's so soothing to be around running water; it's the ultimate detoxifier. When water can't flow, it builds up and becomes stagnant. The same is true of your energy. It takes a lot of effort to hold on to worries—so let them go. Ruminating serves absolutely no purpose; it only keeps you from feeling light and joyful right now. Send those worries some love and let amazonite's clarifying energy wash them away. Since string-of-pearls is in a continuous state of flow, too, it teaches you to get your spirit moving. Sing, dance, take a walk; put your life-force in motion before it turns into restlessness or concern. What do you need to let go of so you can breathe easy again?

Well-Balanced

When you can't decide between the warmth of a citrine and the cool vibes of an amethyst, let nature be the tiebreaker and buy yourself an ametrine. Ametrines are well-balanced crystals with the attributes of both, and a signature energy that's stress reducing, calming, and empowering. It has the potential to create harmony wherever you feel off-center.

ZZ plant is the low-maintenance, modern houseplant you should try if you're not a fan of big, leafy shapes or willowy fronds. Its perfectly placed oval leaflets are supported by a green tapered stem and act like an ensemble, with no one leaf pulling focus from the others. ZZ plant has a balanced aesthetic and uses its resources efficiently, storing water in its succulent leaves and thriving in low light. Rather than producing a flower (which is rare), ZZ plant conserves its energy and focuses on keeping its leaves healthy and evergreen. ZZ plant is not a multitasker, which allows it to be the most carefree plant possible.

THE VIBE

How do you balance work and life? (Asking for a friend.) First of all, there is no such thing as "balance." You have to let that concept go. When you are overly focused on achieving equilibrium, you're more likely to stumble. We can expect perfection and balance only in the natural world, so take that pressure off yourself and appreciate it when you see it in plants and crystals. It's better to calm your energy and work on feeling *centered*. Finding your center means that you will never feel overwhelmed by life. ZZ plant teaches you to use your time wisely, because when you multitask, the most important things you want to do tend to suffer. Ametrine holds the properties of both citrine and amethyst so well that you don't have to worry about creating your own balance. Let the crystal remove from your shoulders the feeling that you have to be perfect at all times. Now you can bring a calm, optimistic energy to everything you do. Focus on doing what brings you the greatest sense of peace. If you need to let go of obligations that are bumming you out, go for it. If you want to take the day off work to spend time with your friends and family, *do it*. ZZ plant and ametrine have everything worked out so there's no need to put pressure on yourself.

CHAPTER TWO

You've Got This

Hello, Rainbow

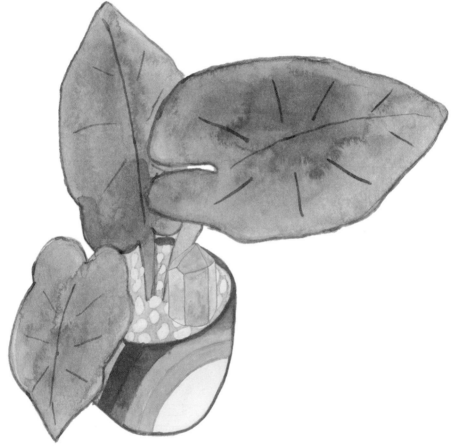

Blue apatite is an opaque crystal with colors ranging from cerulean to azure blue. Its pristine energy and watery color make apatite excellent to work with if you need more direction about your purpose. Blue apatite clears emotions like uncertainty and confusion, which can hold you back from reaching your highest potential. The dynamic current of water energy that lives within its structure will motivate you and help create goals with renewed clarity and deeper insight.

Displaying heart-shaped foliage that looks ancient, elephant ear plant has big energy, like its namesake. Elephant ear's powerful growth capabilities encourage you to think about your own goals and embrace them without apprehension of failure. Its larger-than-life personality makes it a great addition to any outdoor jungle, and it will help you create new opportunities and welcome them with excitement that matches the size of its leaves. If you're feeling unsure and worried about your future, elephant ear's wide, nurturing leaves will catch you in a loving embrace.

THE VIBE

If you feel like you're long overdue for some personal growth and abundance, just affirm: "Hello, Rainbow!" A rainbow isn't deterred by a little stormy weather, nor does it ask for permission to soar high above the earth, so neither should you. It's time to level up and embrace the notion that anything and everything is possible. Blue apatite helps you zero in on your dreams with precision while the spirit of elephant ear inspires you to pursue your loftiest goals with confidence. It's not enough to sit back and wait for blessings to appear; this soulmate match will encourage you to make things happen. Once you discover your true purpose and take inspired action to build your future, it's a colorful adventure that never ends. You may live under the stars, but never forget to soar above the rainbows!

Supercharged You

Rainbow aura quartz expresses the same vibrancy as an aurora borealis, with flashes of colors that are just as diverse and impressive. These exceptional colors are not naturally occurring; they result from plain quartz crystals made more brilliant with a thin coating of gold or titanium, thus becoming high-vibrational superstars that cannot hide their brilliance. A rainbow aura quartz will help you make a quantum leap, soothe tough emotions, and replace them with serenity and self-confidence. Its multicolored facets also encourage you to take pride in your gifts and use them for good.

Monsteras are well known in the botanical world for having slouchy, tropical leaves and reliable growth. It hits all of the superlatives: "best," "most popular," and "most photogenic," and this statement plant has been celebrated in the last few years because of its unusual leaf shape and deep green color. Monstera's perforated leaves are actually an adaptation because of harsh weather conditions in its native environment, the tropical forests of southern Mexico. Wind and rain toss the leaf about, and as the leaf grows, perforations form so that there's less surface area to be tormented by the weather. These perforations make the leaf even lovelier. Monsteras teach you that sometimes allowing yourself to evolve under inclement conditions can help you become the best version of yourself.

THE VIBE

Change is empowering. Sometimes you just need support to make small shifts that will help you become the supercharged version of yourself. Maybe you want to let go of anxiety or be a better friend? A little introspection will show you where you need to apply more mindfulness to your life. Rainbow aura quartz's reflective facets help with self-reflection and give you the courage you need to make those tweaks, and its brilliant energy will help you feel more confident about what you want. Remember, monstera shows us that growth and change are beautiful. Expansion and self-improvement only help you stand in your personal power and adapt to life's challenges. Rainbow aura quartz and monstera should be part of your high-vibrational activation kit, here to remind you that you are solid gold.

Like a Boss

Citrine is success in solid form. And who knew success was so pretty? Saffron, marigold, lemon, burnished honey—these are just some of the ombré variations you can expect when looking for a citrine of your own. The colors won't impact the power of the crystal, so choose the shade that makes you feel happiest. When you pick it up, your citrine should feel powerful, with the warmth of the sun in its faceted edges. Citrine supercharges everything around you with empowering energy that fully supports your endeavors. If you're ready to create new opportunities, look for citrine points or double-terminated versions, instead of tumbled stones. The terminated point will direct a current of energy, like a ray of sunlight, and soon you'll find yourself manifesting the success and abundance you crave.

The cast-iron plant is dependable and tough as nails, much like its elemental namesake, iron. The sturdy plant's thick, paddle-shaped, dark olive leaves bear a strong resemblance to a peace lily, minus the flower. It stays evergreen and looks oh-so-modern in a concrete planter. This is the perfect houseplant if you want something that thrives with minimal care and will still be there for you with healthy, green leaves. Fortitude vibrates through its stems. In fact, novice plant parents who want to pass as responsible plant parents should make cast-iron their top plant pick.

THE VIBE

Any multihyphenate will tell you if you honor your passions, they turn into your purpose, and that's when you'll find success. Achievement milestones happen when you're living your soul's destiny. Working toward that goal takes hard work, passion, and good vibes. Cast-iron plant and citrine are great mentors to keep you motivated throughout your journey. Draw on citrine's abundant, sunny energy to nurture your dreams, as well as its amplification qualities and everlasting power, like the sun. Can a crystal be a content strategist? It can when it's citrine! When you work with citrine, you will find yourself in the creative flow with one stellar idea after another. Cast-iron plant will help your dreams come to fruition by encouraging you to work hard and stay focused on steady gains. Its paddle-shaped leaves remind you that you have the ability to sail through obstacles in your path without losing sight of your goals. Don't wait for a big break. Break through and find your own path. You've got this.

Endless Bummer

Tourmaline is noteworthy for its elongated, faceted shape and sequential bands of color in blues, greens, and pinks. You'll also find single-color stones in a multitude of shapes and hues. What makes tourmaline exceptional is that each color variance carries a different energetic frequency. These distinctions are subtle and contribute to the energy signature of tourmaline as a whole. Overall, tourmaline encourages you to look for the bright spots in your life when you're feeling down and helps you connect to gratitude and love.

Is stromanthe gorgeous, or what? The palette of blush tones, green, and cream in its variegated leaves just might inspire you to redecorate your entire house to match. You could spend hours admiring the variegated pattern and totally miss out on the unexpected twist: the underside of each leaf is tinged in a robust merlot color, confirming that it's possible to be jealous of a plant with perfect highlights and lowlights. Maybe we love stromanthe so much because it's delightful to find pink where you expect only green. Discoveries like this create rich experiences and teach you that there are endless surprises if you make the commitment to look for them.

THE VIBE

When life seems like one bummer after another, happy moments start feeling distant, and toxic emotions, like disappointment, become the norm. It's possible to transition from disappointment to gratitude if you

learn to shift your focus and look for a bright side. Stromanthe teaches that examining something from a different angle yields positive rewards, while colorful tourmaline helps remove burdensome negativity that keeps you from feeling grateful. Center your gaze on one tourmaline color at a time and let its energy work on you in stages. Blue tourmaline calms your field and alleviates stress. Green tourmaline prepares you to receive by opening your heart, and pink tourmaline envelops you with love, so you'll discover things to be thankful for. Soon you'll experience more grace, feel more lively—and those bummer feelings will be a distant memory.

Adulting Made Easy

Moonstones glow like a Bob Ross sunset, their soft incandescence both soothing and mesmerizing. The smooth, pearly surface is nearly opaque but still lets you catch a glimpse of the celestial deposits that glow from within. Holding a moonstone creates a feeling of deep peace and harmony. It's a tool to add ease and grace to wherever you're experiencing stress due to responsibilities weighing you down or apprehension about your future. Moonstone is like coconut oil for your soul—it has an application for every stressor and challenge.

The African violet has an innocence and strength that's reflected in the balance between its graceful bloom and sturdy, verdant leaves. Violets add a sweet energy to any space, and you're most likely to see varieties with pink, blue, or purple flowers. This plant is well-suited to life indoors because of its shallow roots and easygoing nature. Having a low-maintenance plant is great, but that doesn't mean you can avoid giving it the care it needs and still expect to enjoy its beauty. African violets flourish under the right conditions, as long as you give them the right amount of sunshine and water. They're a constant reminder to nurture what's important.

THE VIBE

Being good at adulting is a superpower. No one prepared you for this; no one told you all of your money would be spent on student loans and that the only reliable way to manage your life would be with bulleted journal to-do lists. The highs and lows of adulthood create self-doubt, panic, and stress. It's hard not to lose focus and stay motivated when there is no end to everything you have to take responsibility for. Before you spin out, take a breath. Moonstone will stop you from spiraling with a soft energy that's evenhanded and serene, and its starlike glow will guide you to take positive action in any areas where you lack self-reliance. African violets remind you to be mindful and responsible if you want to see positive results. Bringing this pair into your life will help lessen the burdens of adulthood and encourage you to build a strong foundation for lifelong satisfaction.

Abundance Hero

Pyrite is pure bounty. It's the gold standard of minerals when you cannot afford an actual bar of gold. Chunks of pyrite resemble craggy boulders and have substantial weight for their size, and that tough, metallic luster deflects negativity and attracts luck. Pyrite's light recharges your potential when you feel doubt and clears any blockages you have concerning bounty. In short, it's an energetic charging station for your potential. You can watch the sky and make a wish on a shooting star—or you can get a pyrite and create the same sort of magic every day.

Jade pothos may be the carnation of the houseplant world, but don't discount it. It's a lovely and dependable plant that has so much to offer. That humble demeanor holds a huge secret: pothos has abundance-wattage unlike any other plant out there. To wit: this vine-y babe has an uncanny ability to attract good fortune. Behind every CEO is the jade pothos she sometimes forgets to water but that supports her ability to command prosperity nonetheless. Jade pothos has a crown of great, generous leafy greens, which have a curvature that resembles part of an infinity symbol. Goal-oriented pothos grows toward the light because it loves to sunbathe.

THE VIBE

You are a magnificent being of infinite energy and abundance. It's important for you to know this. Your life is already filled with so much.

When you take notice of everything you have and feel grateful for it, you understand just how blessed you are. This awareness will help you align with the frequency of prosperity so you can welcome more of it into your day-to-day. Jade pothos and pyrite are living affirmations that are happy to help you. Place the two near your workspace to hold an intention for that plentitude. Jade pothos encourages you to set goals and pyrite's golden energy helps you manifest what you want. This powerful duo will release any fears you have about abundance and replace them with golden energy.

Positively Golden

Rutilated quartz is positively golden, literally! Honey-colored inclusions adorn the stone in beautiful patterns that enhance its beauty and energy signature. Smooth, tumbled stones in varying sizes and color variations have a warm and inviting glow. Rutilated quartz may cause you to believe in yourself and open your heart to find out what makes your soul happy. Soon, you'll be looking for ways to share that excitement with those around you.

Sunburst succulents are horticultural gems that brighten green gardens like colorful otomi prints. Booming, generous rosettes explode

in tricolor shades of green, yellow, and sandstone. Sunbursts are beautiful and dependable succulents that dapple the landscape with an abundantly joyful glow that makes a big impact. Work with the plant's energy if you feel called to give back but you're not sure what you have to offer.

THE VIBE

When you give back, you create a current of positivity that shimmers like gold for someone in need. Approaching life with a grateful heart and being mindful about where you can lend a hand is nourishing to your soul. You don't have to save the world, but let your passion drive you to find small ways to be kind. It's contagious once you start, and your generosity creates golden threads that light the way for others to do the same. Rutilated quartz will inspire you with its upbeat, golden energy, and it reminds you that you have the potential to create a big impact, no matter the size of your kind gesture. Sunburst succulents teach you to be bright and remind you that you always have something to offer, even if it's simply a warm and inviting hug to someone. Plants and crystals give so much with loving energy and will inspire you to hold space for kindness and generosity in your life.

Don't Overthink It

Being in the presence of a smoky quartz is instantly calming. You might even notice a weight being lifted from your shoulders. The hazy crystal acts like charcoal, absorbing toxic emotions and negativity so that you stay clear, light, and carefree. It is in tune with earth's resonance and is happy to share it with you so you can get rooted, like a tree, into the earth. Learning this skill creates a solid foundation if you want to begin a meditation practice.

The energy feels different in the desert, as high temperatures and dry conditions are activating and a little overwhelming. Nature has a way of balancing all things and created barrel cactus to ground this electric sensibility back into the earth. Its short stature and natural dome shape make it an anchor of stability. Work with barrel cactus if you're prone to overthinking and want to master feeling grounded.

THE VIBE

Having an overactive mind can make you feel untethered, anxious, and indecisive. Discovering how to ground yourself helps you gain peace and transforms your entire life into a walking meditation. Focusing on barrel cactus's dense form will bring your attention to your own body. Are you taking slow, restorative breaths? Where are you holding tension? Feel into it—and then release it. Smoky quartz is right there to remove those negative emotions from your field. Together, barrel cactus and smoky quartz direct your energy into the earth, so you feel stability beneath your feet. Earth's got you, like the dependable and loving mama she is. With enough practice, you will always be aware of your physical and emotional status and make adjustments to stay in your grounded center.

Get the Fries

What's the deal with this cute yellow crystal that looks like citrine but isn't citrine? Lemon quartz is an absolute spark of joy that's loaded with citrusy, delicious energy. Citrines have a distinct, burnished color and lemon quartz are, well, lemon-y. Actual lemons are naturally tasty and fragrant, and lemon quartz has a similar energy in crystalline form. Use lemon quartz to stimulate your appetite, help you receive abundance, and increase your vitality. You get all of the benefits of a lemon, without the tartness.

Burro's tail is a sweet succulent that looks as if it's been piped on like icing, and its hard-to-resist jadeite hues make it a delightful plant. Its trailing stems start out as perfect star shapes and grow into satisfying ropes that look like macramé creations. This slouchy plant needs plenty of space as it grows and is best suited for suspended planters. Burro's tail loves water and sunlight, and will teach you to appreciate life's sweet moments. Watching this ornamental plant thrive is guaranteed to make you hungry for more succulents.

THE VIBE

It's OK to enjoy life! Many people forget and need a reminder. Relax, take your vacation days, listen to your favorite music, and get the fries while you're at it. These are some of the things that make life awesome. You may feel a little selfish if you're not in work/busy mode all the time, but give yourself a break. Being too restrictive can create more emptiness and more tension. Who needs that? Seeking out joy will only help you attract more abundant experiences. Burro's tail teaches about abundance with its thick cords of succulent leaves, and you'll see that abundance is *beautiful*. Similarly, finding reasons to enjoy every day and be cheerful is easy when you work with lemon quartz's sunny energy.

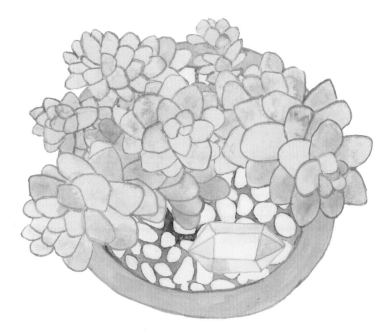

Your Order Has Been Shipped

If you know your crystals, then you've heard that aventurine is a quartz with a low-key luster. You know when your favorite beauty store gives out samples of a fancy milky seaweed cleanser? That's kind of what an aventurine looks like—seafoam green, milky, with a hint of sheen. When you hold one in your hand, you're almost tempted to add water, massage it into your face, and rinse. Aventurine creates joy and luck, and makes you feel optimistic. So it *is* kind of like a face cleanser that gives you a refreshed glow.

Fiddle-leaf fig trees are no longer just trending; they're a staple, like the blue jeans of houseplants. (If anyone tries to tell us otherwise, we will chain ourselves to our fiddle-leaf figs in protest.) Fiddle-leaf figs love the spotlight and thrive in bright light, and they will reward you with broad, healthy leaves that are glossy on one side and have a parchment finish on the other. This green scene-stealer will upstage your other plants with its showy display and storied looks—the years of buzz and excitement have definitely gone to its leaves and trunk. It's important to show respect for fiddle-leafs; if not for them, would the houseplant craze have even started?!

THE VIBE

"Your order has been shipped" is the most exciting phrase ever. Pure bliss, right? If only you could bottle that excitement and apply it all over your life. You can dream or you can order a fiddle-leaf fig tree and an aventurine crystal. Anticipate that which will bring you greater bliss and adventure. A fiddle-leaf fig's inflated energy creates buzz and its apple-green leaves revitalize any space, while optimistic aventurine creates an environment where you always have something to look forward to. These two create a hype that makes you feel like something awesome is on its way. Life has endless moments to feel cheerful about, which may or may not involve shopping for plants and crystals and waiting with eagerness for that delivery to arrive.

Tiny & Mighty

Desert island crystal time: your secluded Airbnb adventure has turned into a flop. Which crystal do you take with you? A. Celestite, B. Amethyst, or C. Tourmaline? The answer is A! You need a lot of help trusting when things feel out of control, and celestite is your best resource. It is found inside geodes and has muted blue crystal clusters that look like glittering stars. This crystal will help you relax and learn to trust again if you're feeling worried or holding on to tough emotions.

Budget-friendly ivy is a determined plant. This evergreen is confident in its ability to flourish even under harsh conditions. In the wild, ivy provides good ground cover and will grow over every rock and tree trunk in its path. Ivy adapts and exceeds expectations with reliable growth and beauty, and you can trust it to thrive with even minimal care.

THE VIBE

The ability to surrender in the face of the unknown is a difficult lesson to master. "Trust the journey" is one of the most loaded phrases on earth. Does it fill you with peace or doubt? Probably doubt. If you have a hard time keeping the faith because of past hurts or sad experiences, it's OK to rely on a little energetic support. Celestial celestite helps soften your energy so that you feel calm and can breathe easy, knowing that everything will work out in your favor. Ivy has confidence to spare and can teach you a lot about self-reliance, and the two together provide a safe bubble of energy you can trust-fall into. Life requires patience and trust. Just know that everything will turn out better than you expected.

Truth Halo

Kyanite teaches you to stand in your power and truth. When you work with kyanite, you will speak from your soul with an authority that's loving but firm. It will help you resolve patterns where you didn't have good boundaries and were giving away your power. With its calming energy nearby, you will have the confidence to communicate your needs, making it the best crystal for self-expression and healing.

Yucca plants are super-hardy, drought-tolerant plants that love the desert life. They're sort of intimidating, with pointed leaves and a thick, fibrous cane but make wonderful houseplants when you learn more about them. Those long leaves stretch out to create a boundary of good energy. Consider adding one to your home if you love desert-scape décor. Yuccas are happy inside as long as they have sunlight and enough space to grow. They need a sturdy planter because they're prone to falling over if they get too tall. Of course, if your yucca plant keeps falling over, it's outgrown its surroundings and should be moved outside for more space. In fact, it can teach you a lot about moving on when the current conditions aren't supporting you.

THE VIBE

Protecting your boundaries isn't a defensive act, it's loving and an important part of self-care. You can keep your heart open when you have robust boundaries. If you feel drained, you might be out of alignment with work, friends, or family. Are you doing more for others than for yourself? It's time to reexamine your relationships and maybe even walk away from them if you feel like they're breaching your comfort zone. How many times can a yucca plant fall over until you realize it simply needs more room? The same principle applies to you. You cannot be constantly doing for others or being taken advantage of, falling over all the time. Yucca teaches you to do what's best for you, with confidence. Kyanite helps eliminate past resentments held in your body where you were giving away your power. The crystal helps you to express your needs without feeling bad about it. The most important relationship you have is with yourself, so make sure you're getting the care you need.

CHAPTER THREE

No Bad Days

Homebody

The best crystals hold colorful spectrums, and rainbow fluorite balances many colors in gentle harmony. It all works in unison without looking too messy. This peaceful crystal settles the energy of your home, and you as well, so it's great to work with if you long for more peace in your life. It will help you take a centered approach to whatever areas need the most attention.

Echeveria succulents are a favorite among plant ladies because they make elegant additions to pebbled container gardens. Their symmetrical rosettes in green, blue, yellow, pink, and purple encourage you to appreciate the allure of simplicity and a well-balanced design. Echeverias are grounded and chill, and add high-end beauty to every container garden. They also teach you to appreciate the peace that a perfect design can create.

THE VIBE

If your home is feeling boring and lackluster, now is the time to declutter and decorate. An organized home is important for your well-being because you need a place that invites you to relax and recharge. Tidy and neat, echeverias teach that there's beauty in order, while rainbow fluorite will motivate you to get to work and restore some much-needed harmony. It's tough to start home projects if you have big goals and rainbow fluorite will give you the push you need to clear out the sluggishness that's been holding you back. This duo will inspire you to turn your home into a living Pinterest board and give your bookcase the ROY G BIV treatment (to match that rainbow fluorite). Connect with your inner homebody. The result will be a sanctuary that you'll never want to leave, and the one rule is SWEATPANTS ONLY.

I Love a Good Sheet Mask

Apophyllite is your glow-to crystal for relaxation inspiration, and its appearance of crystalized sugar clusters will satisfy your sweet tooth with one look. It sparkles with a platinum iridescence and feminine energy. The bubbly beauty's clusters of iridescent hues may make you feel more energized because of its high vibration. Stress and tension *cannot exist* in apophyllite's presence, so keep it in your bedroom or bathroom and create a self-care sanctuary.

Aloe vera is your beauty touchstone, there to remind you to stay hydrated and moisturize. This self-care staple has healing qualities that go way beyond skin care benefits. Its sage-green leaves store water and a healing gel that has thousands of uses. Aloe vera does well in rocky gardens because it loves sunlight and won't wrinkle from sun damage. It has a protective and nurturing energy, and guides you to take good care of yourself.

THE VIBE

Self-care is a misunderstood practice. It might seem selfish to focus on *numero uno*, but putting yourself first is a form of respect. Self-care is the love language of your soul, and will increase your well-being and happiness. Think about the simple act of wearing a sheet mask. You cannot be productive while wearing one; it's a basic law of physics. Stress cannot reach you in that dewy state, so instead your thoughts turn to baths, naps, essential oils, journaling, avocados, and rolling of

every kind (face and foam). The world melts away for a bit while you indulge. You're already halfway there just by reading this, but aloe vera and apophyllite will nudge you along even more: aloe vera encourages you to put your well-being first, while apophyllite's strong presence clears away any guilt you may have around doing just that. If self-care has been difficult for you in the past, work with these elements so that it becomes a regular practice.

Sunday Naps

Falling asleep to the sound of crashing waves is a most delightful experience. Don't stress if you're landlocked; you can still experience the energy of the sea in gemstone form with ocean jasper. The stone's predominant colors are blue, green, and cream, and its pattern looks like swirling surf, with algae and kelp forests below. Ocean jasper's tranquility invites you to stop overthinking and inspires you to dream. It's a fantastic tool if restful sleep has been eluding you, as it cleanses away stress and grounds your energy so you can fall asleep with ease.

A mini agave plant tucked into a ceramic planter is just about the sweetest houseplant around. Agave is mellow and grows at a slow pace. Its layers of frosty, blue-green leaves form concentric star shapes that radiate serenity, inviting you to let go of your worries and send them away on a shooting star.

THE VIBE

Nothing tastes as good as sleep feels. A restful night is critical for your soul and your overall well-being. When is the last time you enjoyed an impromptu nap? If you can't remember when, stop denying yourself sleep and take a nap! Weekend naps are the best, but restorative sleep is well within reach at all times when you work with agave plant and ocean jasper. Place this combo near your bed or a couch and let ocean jasper's calming energy splash you playfully with a sense of serenity and help you relax. Agave's geometrical symmetry will assist in restoring your natural circadian rhythm as well. Celebrate sleep and see how great you start to feel when you bring agave and ocean jasper into your space. Resting sets the stage for deep healing and release, so don't let your zzzs suffer anymore.

Cosmic Reboot

Bluebird azurite is an all-purpose stone with the ability to clear blockages, help release limiting beliefs, bring greater clarity, and raise your vibration. Bluebird is a mixture of electric azure blue, green malachite, and copper, and if you're seeking a reboot, the stone will upgrade your energy on multiple levels. Bluebird's energy is more powerful than other blue stones, like topaz, aquamarine, and apatite, because of the depth of its color.

A good plant haul is when you bring home a round-leaf calathea. It has major beauty with dramatic, cabbage-like foliage. When the sun sets, its broad green leaves fold up and open again at sunrise, a natural mechanism to conserve energy in the evening. Like humans, the plant needs to power down and recharge at the end of a long day. Calathea teaches you to honor your own natural rhythms and your need to recuperate. The next morning, its leaves open again with the sun, and that nightly reset helps calathea bring fresh energy into your home.

THE VIBE

A cosmic reboot is a fresh start when your self-care routine isn't meeting your needs anymore. You might feel tired and disconnected, and not know what to do to feel vibrant again. Sometimes the best way to refresh is to stop trying and do nothing. Let round-leaf calathea and bluebird azurite do all the work instead. Take a break and power down like calathea when you're exhausted and overwhelmed, and let azurite upgrade your operating system with a gentle intensity, clearing out any blockages. Working with these elements is just the boost you need to run smoothly again. You water your plants and charge your crystals in the sun; make time to honor your own needs, too.

Golden Hour

Selenite's intense inner glow can appear opaque white, lavender, or blue. It looks like it was made from pure light that's been frozen in solid form. Selenite holds immense energy and can actually cleanse and recharge other crystals. The stone brings uplift and refreshing energy to your home much like palo santo or sage. When you're around high-vibe selenite, you might feel like you have permanent post-workout glow.

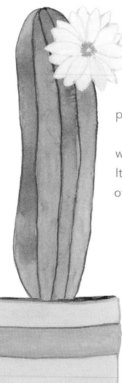

Cereus is a slender, column-shaped cactus with a dazzling flower that blooms in the evening. Its lotus-like flower is white and yellow with hints of neon green shades. Cereus grows wild in the desert and you can always find one at your local nursery or botanical garden. Small varieties will fill your space with happy, vibrant feels. What cereus lacks in leaves, it makes up for in floral energy—not to mention that a flower that blooms during golden hour is very special indeed.

THE VIBE

When the sun starts to set, it casts a brilliant glow. Everything looks better during golden hour and it gives you something to look forward to after a long day. How wonderful that you're always assured of a breathtaking sunrise and an equally amazing sunset. It's a beautiful transition and an opening act to what comes next: stargazing. During golden hour, take a moment to reflect on what made you happy that day and find something to look forward to tomorrow. Selenite's powerful glow reminds you that there is *always* something to feel positively about. Night-blooming cereus will brighten up your home and turn you into a dreamer. If a cactus can produce a flower on one special evening, then you have every reason to be an eternal optimist. Your mind-set creates your experience, so just remember that everything looks better when it's golden.

I Feel Pretty

Natural pink opal is a rarefied gemstone with bubble-gum good looks. It comes in various terra-cotta shades and millennial pink tones, leaving no wonder as to why it's so popular. Basically, it's beauty personified, with a rustic appeal that doesn't adhere to the traditional standards of other crystals. Work with pink opal if you desire a stone with gentle, feminine energy that will help you connect to your heart-space.

Hibiscus plants give us a whole new reason to be in love with plants. Just look at what nature is capable of doing with a little effort. Hibiscus flowers can be found in single colors, like pink, orange, yellow, and white, while other varieties display whimsical mixtures that you usually only find in pigmented makeup palettes. Hibiscus hits the sweet spot of tropical and fragrant, with an evocative scent that's not too cloying. Big botanical style and hard-to-resist charm make hibiscus the unexpected houseplant you should take a chance on.

THE VIBE

What makes you beautiful isn't what you wear or your eight-step skin care routine, it's your natural radiance. When you add pink opal and hibiscus to your home, you can't help but feel pretty. Nature manifests the exquisiteness of her soul in plants and crystals, and hibiscus is one of Mother Earth's most attractive babies. It inspires to celebrate your own glamour, like the flower you are. Pink opal encourages you to live life without filters and feel confident in your unadorned state. The stone has a universally flattering energy that feels good on everyone. Every plant lady and crystal mama is beautiful, especially you.

Wellness Warrior

Hemimorphite resembles pristine glacial water that's been preserved in an ancient aqueduct and unearthed millions of years later. It's the purest blue you've ever seen. Just looking at it will make you thirsty.

(*Pause for a hydration break*)

Now that you're back, hemimorphite gets its blue color from the mineral zinc. Zinc keeps you healthy and strong, which is why hemimorphite has immune-boosting capabilities. If you're experiencing "health helplessness," hemimorphite will help you create new habits and healthy changes.

Green velvet alocasia is not swiss chard, but the resemblance is uncanny. This humidity-loving plant has a velvety texture and blue-green color. Since alocasia is a tropical plant, it does best when in a kitchen or bathroom. It's also health-conscious and loves plenty of clean water and indirect sunlight. When you see how healthy alocasia can be with the proper care, it will inspire you to improve your own wellness routine.

THE VIBE

Sharing your space with plants and crystals improves your spiritual and physical well-being. They create a healing environment for you to tap into your soul-guided wellness. An energetic shot of green velvet alocasia and hemimorphite will jump-start a new routine. They nourish

you by filling your cells with light, transforming you into a wellness warrior who thrives on clean foods and water, robust energy, and ripe avocados. Alocasia inspires you to figure out a plan of action to make your health a priority and serves as a daily visual reminder to eat your greens. Hemimorphite clears the energy from unhealthy habits and helps you establish better ones. You'll have all the encouragement you need to make the necessary leaps to improve your well-being in the long run.

Let's Do This

Natural red hematite looks like a rugged mountain gem—tough and brawny, with a high intensity that will increase your willpower. Work with a terminated crystal point to increase your motivation and stamina. Hematite is fierce and iron is what makes the crystal blush and resemble the rosy-cheeked glow you get after a hot yoga class. Add a red hematite crystal to your collection if you want to increase your strength and physical energy because it contains the power of a thousand workouts in its form.

Dolphin plant is teeming with motion and playful energy. Dolphin-shaped succulents leap and tumble over cascading vines in imaginary surf with an excitement and joy that will inspire you to get moving. If you find yourself in a workout rut and in need of fitspiration, dolphin plant's spry energy will give you a fresh start. The water-filled succulent will also help you cool down

after your workouts with a visual reminder to stay hydrated—you amazing but dehydrated goddess!

THE VIBE

A well-curated collection of activewear can give you the confidence to crush your workouts. But, if your workout style is more yoga naps (that's when you spend the entire class napping in savasana pose) and less foam rolling, then it takes more than a trendy pair of tie-dye leggings to motivate you. Finding the motivation to achieve your fitness goals is shockingly simple when you work with high-performance red hematite and dolphin plant. Basic workouts can be boring, so dolphin plant will inspire you to mix things up and find something that pumps you up, like your favorite playlist. Warm up with red hematite's athletic might and uplift your energy so you can make the most of your workouts. Natural personal trainers such as red hematite and dolphin plant are important parts of your fit-evolution, taking your fitness routine from "Maybe later" to "Let's do this!"

Air Space

Himalayan salt is good for you. You can use it daily to season your food, but it also has purifying qualities and disperses negative ions in the air when heated. Not only that, Himalayan salt produces uplifting negative ions just like the ocean or a waterfall does. If you crave the serenity of water, a salt lamp or a votive can boost your mood with the same energy by releasing heated salt particles into the air to get to work like tiny superheroes, improving air quality and creating feel-good energy.

Snake plant is a working plant that cleans the air by filtering airborne toxins through its sturdy leaves. Its organic air filtration won't run up your electric bill or keep you awake with an annoying hum. Snake plant makes your space feel fresh and look pretty with its patterned dark green leaves. It adapts well to every environment, so there are no limits as to where you can place it. A dusty room with indirect light is a great spot for a snake plant, as it will go to work cleaning up the air and making a refreshing space for you to enjoy. One of the perks of being a plant lady is that when you take care of your plants, they also take care of you!

THE VIBE

You've defined your style and decorated your home, but how's your air space feeling? The area between your campaign dresser and woven headboard needs the most attention, as that's where dust and other pollutants can linger, causing respiratory irritations. No, thank you! Purifying the air is easy when you combine a snake plant with a Himalayan salt crystal. Enjoy better air quality without having to replace the filters on your HVAC. Snake plant's stalwart leaves clean the air and release oxygen, and Himalayan salt picks up the slack with those negative ions to neutralize anything you don't want in your lungs. You'll find yourself wanting to spend all of your time near your snake plant and Himalayan salt crystal. Natural air fresheners are always your best bet for a healthier home.

Pop-Up Shop

No, rainbow lattice sunstone is not a limited-edition crystal. Rather, it's a naturally occurring sunstone embedded with metallic lattice inclusions that derive their color from different minerals. The technical term for this glittery effect is "aventurescence." Don't worry, it's not the type of glitter that sticks to everything and makes a mess. Think of it as cosmic glitter that has the power to uncover your hidden creative talents and inspire you better than your favorite Pinterest influencer. Creativity, encouragement, manifestation, and self-acceptance are just a few qualities that rainbow lattice sunstone embodies, making it the ultimate if you want to raise your ingenuity quotient without doubting your abilities.

The leaves of a fishtail palm drape elegantly in midair like the skirt of a flamenco dancer waiting for the music to start. There is motion conveyed in its stillness. Its richly colored and textured leaves have accordion-like folds resembling crepe paper cutouts made by pinking shears. If Mother Nature sold plants at a pop-up shop, they would look a lot like fishtail palm—a flamenco-skirted, crepe-paper creation that epitomizes vitality and joy.

THE VIBE

Creativity is the soul's highest form of expression. Using your visionary gifts, no matter what you are drawn to make, relieves stress and sends bliss out into the world. You can visit a pop-up shop to experience

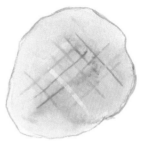

innovation in person (fun products, cool concepts, and avant-garde vibes), or you can add a fishtail palm and rainbow lattice sunstone to your space.

Fishtail palm nudges you to be free, dance, and look to nature for inspiration. Express yourself enthusiastically. If you're looking for motivation to do so, sunstone's orderly lattice configuration will help you determine what you want to create and save you from the turmoil of a DIY excursion down the social media rabbit hole that leaves you feeling exhausted instead of inspired. Now's the time to apply some of that cosmic glitter, too. Sunstone tells you to play and let go of any criticism that may be holding you back from expressing your talents. Now that your creativity is fully supported, what will you create?

Sweatpants Are the Best Pants

Chalcedony is a challenge to pronounce but a joy to be around. Its energy is tranquil and so is its palette, with pale, almost barely there shades of lavender, pink, blue, and green that make it a favorite of the Zen crowd. The stone's glassine finish and soft magnetism capture your full attention. Everything about chalcedony is peaceful, with the ability to make even the most crabby individual feel blissed out. Choose a raw stone if you want to experience its natural, unfiltered state, but a high-polished cabochon is also very appealing.

Think outside the ceramic planter and give blue star fern a chance to impress you with its modern look and relaxed sensibility. Unlike traditional ferns that feel very uptight, blue stars are completely chill, with ribbon-like teal leaves that make careless arrangements of them-selves, like perfectly messy hair. Blue star ferns are too busy being themselves to notice if a leaf is out of place. Adopting that wild and carefree attitude is very liberating and will inspire you to do the same.

THE VIBE

#lifegoal: Find sheets that double as pajamas and reach the highest level of hygge possible.

If you love comfort and everything cozy, then you know there is no limit to how relaxed you can be. There's always a deeper state of peace to achieve if you really try. Are you good at relaxing, or do you need help? If you need assistance, put on your sweatpants (because they are the best pants) and get yourself a chalcedony and a blue star fern. Learn from blue star fern's carefree leaves and make yourself at home. Find the comfiest surface in your home and make it your lounge. Stretch out or curl up; settle in and feel your cares disappearing. Chal-cedony's soothing presence will activate your parasympathetic ner-vous system, i.e., calm you down. You might find yourself letting out little sighs or yawns, which means it's working. Having a regular relax-ation practice can be a real game changer. Give yourself some down-time and see how awesome you feel.

Flower Crown

An ocean wave cycles through a barrel of energy right before it breaks onto the shore. That single wave holds so much spirit and potential, and some of that same power is part of aquamarine's energetic signature. It has a strong connection to the water, with a crystal-blue color and linear inclusions that convey the motion of a wave in crystalline form. Use this watery energy to cleanse negative emotions, like fear, doubt, and worry, leaving you with strength and confidence that cannot be washed away.

Never underestimate the power of a super bloom, which blankets the desert with vibrant displays in every color and tiny green bundles of prickly cacti that were eager for the moment they could showcase their exquisite flowers. A humble cactus wearing a flower crown is the epitome of confidence. Crown cactus in particular shares a strong bond with the flowers it so proudly shows off. Even with the unrelenting sun and dry weather, crown cactus flourishes under conditions that most plants would find stressful. A flower crown is beautiful but also a symbol of strength and survival.

THE VIBE

Let's call it quits on low-vibrational feelings like self-doubt. A lack of assurance can do a number on your life and self-esteem. When you feel "less than," you are holding yourself back from opportunities and experiences that are integral to your growth. But low confidence can be easily overcome when you work with aquamarine's ultra-cool character and borrow some of crown cactus's confidence. First, imagine a wave of energy washing over you, banishing lower vibrations and uncovering your most courageous self. Aquamarine's tenacity will help you stay in this state, while crown cactus teaches you that a little pressure is nothing to be concerned about. Your capability and strength are unmatched and cannot be deterred by any circumstance. If you actually need to wear a flower crown to remember this, then by all means wear one. It can be a colorful reminder to never doubt yourself again.

CHAPTER FOUR

The Plant & Crystal Diet

Your Daily Podcast

Emeralds are super gorg but also super expensive. You get the same characteristics with an emerald quartz, if you want a deep-green crystal, with money left to buy its plant soul mate. Green stones are associated with the energy of renewal and expansion. They're an abundant source of positivity and will support your personal growth. Emerald quartz also enhances your memory and clears brain fog, keeping you bright as a quartz point. When you work with the crystal, you'll notice that you have more patience and mental focus, too.

Jade plant has a huge fan base because it's reliable and easy to care for. This gal is carefree and thrives no matter what; you'll be able to intuit what it needs like a seasoned plant mom. When you don't have the knowledge to care for a houseplant but your home feels empty without one, get a jade plant, which never fails to impress with its woody stems and a full head of succulent, oval-shaped leaves. Place it wherever you need a dash of green; it will adapt and grow without much nurturing from you.

THE VIBE

What's your learning style? Are you book smart? Or do you prefer podcasts? Discovering new information is an important part of your personal growth. Read compelling books, listen to cool interviews, and dive into interesting topics that give you a fresh perspective on life. Learning should be fun, leading you to discover new aspects of yourself and interests you never knew you had. Jade plant will get the ball rolling by inviting you to take a carefree approach. If a topic doesn't interest you, don't worry about it! Move on and find something else that intrigues you rather than spending precious effort on a topic that doesn't light you up. Emerald quartz will put you in the right mindset to encode that knowledge with increased mental clarity and memory recall. Together, jade plant and emerald quartz encourage you to expand your world and engage in what you love.

Modern Magic

Boulder opals sparkle, physically and metaphysically, due to a high concentration of water-rich silica deposits that reflect light to produce flashes of turquoise, green, pink, and lavender. The ability to transform ordinary light into a whirl of colors is proof that opal is magical, with a high-vibrational resonance. If you peer inside, it looks like an ancient ocean was flash frozen to preserve its uplifting and nurturing energy. Boulder opals are an absolute joy—you can't help but feel that life is enchanted when you hold one in your hand.

Fan palm's tropical silhouette is a mainstay in resort-style décor. Those leafy sunbursts lofted above thick stems make them a solar symbol, and their circular fronds diffuse bursts of energy through their fanlike folds in all directions like fireworks. This shape is an energetic amplifier that will support you in any area where you want transformation. Due to their size, it's best to keep fan palms outside, but smaller ones are happy indoors and will give your space a satisfying dose of booming greenergy. There is no limit to the number of plants you can add to your home (I always say the more, the merrier), but a dramatic fan palm may be all the green you need—for now.

THE VIBE

When delightful things keep happening and you can no longer attribute them to coincidence, you're experiencing modern magic, or synchronicities. Synchronicities are those unexpected, sparkly moments

that break up the monotony and make life rosy. You may find white feathers in your path, you might be thinking of an old friend only to run into them at the farmers' market, or you may be experiencing miracles you never thought possible. If you're ready to experience nothing less than felicitous occurrences, it's time to work with boulder opal and fan palm. Let boulder opal's flash and dazzle create extraordinary experiences in the form of synchronicities. The fan of the fan palm will amplify the energy of the opal and make it more powerful. The synergy between these two is tangible: it vibrates in the air and sends out waves of receptive energy to open the gate for synchronicities to enter.

Free & Clear

Zeolites are aggregates of different minerals that look like molded sugar crystals. The prettiest clusters have multiple pastel colors in their matrices. Visual appeal is one reason that people scatter zeolite around their home as décor, but it's actually a utilitarian crystal that has value beyond its good looks. Check this out: it has been proven to absorb toxins and may even neutralize EMFs, the electric and magnetic fields that are bouncing around us all the time in the form of Wi-Fi and power lines. It can also strengthen your energy field against negativity with its supergrounded vibes.

Spider plant is an underappreciated garden staple that deserves a place in your home. Definitely in the top three "easiest houseplants to care for," its natural fountain shape looks ultra trendy in a simple earthenware planter. Not only that, its elongated leaves purify the air and sweep up EMF pollution. It's true; NASA said so! Keep a spider plant at your workstation or on an elevated stand nearby for the greatest benefit.

THE VIBE

You were a little overzealous with your workspace and now it's a full-fledged tech hub, brimming with productivity—and EMFs. EMFs from your computer and cell phone create low vibrations that don't feel so awesome. Our high-tech lives need a break. It's OK to work with technology—and pretty much impossible not to—as long as you also work with nature. So the next time you're scrolling on your phone for plant-inspo, do yourself a favor and sit near a spider plant and a zeolite. Together, they act like a firewall to absorb and neutralize electronic impurities around you. Instead, you'll notice a bubble of refreshing energy that keeps you motivated and gives you peace of mind, even when you're working hard for hours (or simply seeking out the funniest cat videos on the 'net).

Sacred Saguaro

Raw iolite holds entire galaxies in its mineral inclusions and bright spots of blue, which contrast against deep indigos and draw you in with the same mystery as the night sky.

In general, the more intense the color of a stone, the more wisdom it holds, so it's not surprising that iolite can help you strengthen your connection to your own intuition during meditation. Use it to follow your soul's guidance.

Saguaro cactus is the memory keeper of the desert. Its graceful form holds water encoded with cellular memories of a thousand sunsets and even more natural wisdom. This plant withstands the harsh landscape like a meditating sage, deriving power from within by connecting to its inner strength and peace. When the outer world is in flux, the saguaro grows slowly and appears relatively unchanged from day to day, only blooming when the time is right. The ancient cactus is well-suited to life in the badlands, never compromising its majesty under tough circumstances.

THE VIBE

There are some truths that you must feel with your heart and not your head, and when you connect to your intuition, you live from a place of knowing and not thinking. You understand that the whole universe is inside of you and you have an inherent wisdom that guides you. How cool is that? That inner knowing is your greatest teacher and gift. Saguaro cactus and iolite help quiet your mind so you can access this sagacity of yours. Learn to be a neutral observer like the saguaro, which has firm desert roots but stands apart from the rest of the landscape with its stalwart presence. Saguaro teaches you to be unmoved by the ups and downs of daily life so that you are always connected to an intrinsic well of calm—because that's where your power resides. Iolite will empower you to trust that deep knowledge and tap into your instincts. When you work with these two energies, you will approach life with wisdom and a renewed sense of understanding about your role in the world.

Spirit Animal

What's your spirit animal? Maybe you prefer a spirit crystal, like Australian jasper? The stone is grounding and calming and will help you connect with animals. Rich earth tones, in deep reds and burnished yellows, round out the energy of Australian jasper, and you feel warm and fuzzy in its presence. Incorporate the stone into your regular relaxation practice if you desire more serenity and a calm feeling that only animals can bring.

Peperomia is pet-friendly, super cute, and so easy to care for that you might find yourself adopting more of them. Especially when you find out peperomia is actually a baby rubber plant (aw!). Adorable, lovable peperomias are the golden retrievers of the houseplant club because of their popularity and easygoing, loyal nature. Tiny, round leaves resemble floppy puppy ears, and you may find yourself doting on the plant like you would a sweet pet. Peperomia is low-maintenance and always looks well-groomed—making it the perfect starter plant.

THE VIBE

Animals are our best friends and greatest guides. When we have their best care in mind, they give back absolute love and companionship. They show us how to view the world with unconditional love, how to play and live without worry and be our authentic selves. Animals live in a constant state of awe and are unmoved by the bustle of life. Imagine experiencing life with carefree energy and innocence—what a blessing that would be! You can experience that feeling for yourself when you work with peperomia and Australian jasper. Together, they represent the best qualities of animals. Australian jasper will settle your energy until you feel grounded and deeply connected to animals. You may notice feeling total peace, and full of love and appreciation. Peperomia teaches you to be easygoing and loosen up! Using this soul mate pair will help you operate from a place of total bliss and see how wonderful life can be!

Wanderlust

A single sugilite contains every shade of purple and pink, a color combo that complements its empowering side. Purple gemstones have a rare energy, and sugilite urges you to be free and clears a path for you to explore the world. Its power is rooted in protection, so that wherever life takes you, you will feel peaceful and secure. Every wandress should pack a sugilite on her adventures, so that she is always assured of safe travels and unforgettable experiences.

Oversized is the new minimal, and kentia palm fits that description well with its streamlined leaves and towering form. Living with giant plants may inspire you to plan giant adventures. Wild kentia palms thrive in the subtropical landscape of Lord Howe Island off the coast of Australia but are also content to bring their resort-style energy into the empty corners of your home. Put kentia palm on your wish list if you love tropical plants with fronds that move and dance in the slightest breeze. It displays so much grace that you will quickly consider adopting other megasized plants that are similarly sultry (don't say I didn't warn you).

THE VIBE

The best moments in life usually involve a rolling suitcase and a plane ride. Where does your wild soul want to go? It's time to stop planning etheric trips and start planning actual trips because travel enriches your life with extraordinary moments. Plan your adventures and watch how the universe conspires to make them happen, especially when you work with kentia palm and sugilite. Just being near a kentia palm will give you the travel bug, so be prepared for wanderlust to hit you like a tropical force, and intrepid explorers love sugilite's get-up-and-go attitude. The urge for freedom and peregrination will come on strong, and these two will help you plan an epic journey. Home is where your plants and crystals are, but they won't miss you if you leave for a bit.

Minimal Boho

Sodalite is blue and white, with a faintly vintage-washed appearance. It's composed of salt, mostly, but other minerals balance out its composition for an eclectic look. As we've discussed, salt is the great neutralizer and can clear away negative energy. Work with sodalite if you have trouble with insecurity, making decisions, or want to be more creative. Sodalite clears whatever blockages are keeping you from expressing yourself, so if you want to tackle artistic projects or decorate your home, it will inspire you to do so with a gentle, encouraging nudge.

Is a dragon tree too bold for your home? (No.) This "tree" is actually a traditional houseplant with a striking balance of green-, red-, and pink-colored leaves, as well as a crown of ombré foliage and a braided trunk, making it Mother Nature's fiercest plant. Its slender leaves with tough edges grow in all directions and act like a kinetic amplifier, inspiring you to take chances. It will spruce up the energy of your place with a modern boho look.

THE VIBE

When it's time to upgrade the décor and energy of your space, the way your soul would decorate, you need an editorial approach and a muse. When you decorate your home, one of the most important things to do first is establish a plant and crystal corner. Dragon tree and sodalite will help you along by providing the stimulating boost

that you need to elevate your style and demystify the decorating process. Sodalite's salty energy makes life a little less boring and encourages you to spice up your décor choices. The stone will unblock your creativity and turn you into a true interior designer in no time, while the bold dragon tree asks you to find statement pieces you'll love forever. You may be surprised to discover what you like. Who knew you had a passion for organic elements and celestial ceramics? No matter what you choose, a dragon tree will harmonize everything. Nature is really the best stylist for cultivating a design aesthetic, making your house a home. Remember: when in doubt, sprinkle more plants and crystals throughout.

Matcha-Exhaustion

Just as green sprouts give off a ton of potential energy, it turns out that green crystals do as well. Yes, superfood stones exist and you need one now. Jade's crystalline form resonates at the frequency of abundance, longevity, prosperity, and healing. This spirited crystal is so full of life-force that it can recharge itself *and* other crystals, just by being near them. It's the ultimate adaptogenic gem. Let its gentle and masterful wattage do the same for you.

Wild hosta radiates big charm. Its leaves flood the visual landscape with so much chlorophyll that every shade of green is represented. Its concave leaves capture water to hydrate the plant—an efficient use of design and energy! Larger varieties do best outdoors, but mini versions make perfect roommates, with a vibe that's one part enchanted and one part trendy. Take good care of your hosta and you will enjoy its exuberance for a long time.

THE VIBE

Green wavelengths carry in them the energies of renewal, vibrancy, and well-being—the very forces that propel life forward. That's the basic principle behind why everything green gives you a little zing, like matcha, chlorophyll, spirulina, wheat grass, and chlorella. Try swapping your morning matcha latte for hosta and jade; after all, there's only so much green stuff you can drink until you need a new pick-me-up. Hosta and jade make a potent blend, with bioavailable energy that's exceptional for your soul. Why metabolize caffeine when you can metabolize green light instead? Jade gives off a pure current that matches the resonance of your soul and will bring your system back into harmony. Hosta directs that energy and uses it efficiently, so that you have a steady stream. Give this harmonizing blend a try instead of your usual morning beverages to find yourself bubbling and sparkling like a cool glass of prosecco.

Earth Muse

When a quartz crystal starts to form, sometimes the conditions aren't perfect and it stops growing. When the conditions for growth are suitable again, a new crystal forms over the original, often trapping its colored minerals inside. This is how phantoms are made. Phantom quartz is a radiant ecosystem of minerals and fractals whose inner beauty displays natural cycles of renewal, held inside clear green facets. It's grounded earth wisdom you can see and hold.

Banana palms will happily hold space for you under their protective leaves, which provide shelter from the sun, wind, or rain. If you love robust leaves, add a versatile banana palm to your outdoor space. Since these pups grow quickly, their frayed leaves are a sustainable resource in many regions of the world. And let's not forget that many varieties produce bananas, so you'll always have an endless supply for your smoothie bowls. Getting a selfless and generous banana palm will nurture the part of you that's been asking for more nature.

THE VIBE

Earth muses who embrace the zero-waste life sometimes need additional ground support in the form of plant wisdom and crystal healing. Banana palm and phantom quartz have a soulful relationship that will deepen your connection to Mother Earth and teach you how to live mindfully. They will inspire you to live in a more sustainable way and satisfy your inner eco-goddess with their gorgeous muted tones. Banana palm's nurturing nature reminds you to consider how your daily choices will impact the earth, and its broad and protective leaves will motivate you to make helpful changes, like reducing your plastic usage and supporting green businesses. Phantom quartz's embodiment of the natural cycles of the world might inspire you to plant a seasonal garden or to learn about upcycling. These beauties can teach us a lot about renewal and conscious living, and they're here to remind you that guidance comes in many forms.

Let's Get Alchemical

Clear quartz looks like a fractal of light and is just as powerful. Minimalists love its streamlined look, and crystal fans in general appreciate its high vibration. Some varieties even hold rainbow inclusions in their structure. You can program clear quartz with any intention you want because of its purity, so whether you are seeking love, harmony, or clarity or need assistance with your meditation practice, it's here to help. Use it to clear negative energy from your space, too. Clear quartz is a forceful amplifier, so don't be surprised if its energy comes on strong at first. In time, it will strengthen your aura and you will be a good energetic match.

Umbrella plant stands tall with a sturdy trunk and a dense canopy of glossy leaves, the upper ones slouching protectively to shelter the ones below. Those leaves are green or variegated and cluster together like mini tropical umbrellas. It transforms any empty spaces into a lush indoor jungle. This playful plant matures quickly, often needing to be moved to a larger container every few years. It will evolve with you, supporting your personal and spiritual growth all the while.

THE VIBE

The universe is in a constant flux of transformation and expansion. Change is just energy expressing itself, a variable you can expect and should embrace with open arms. Don't be afraid of change; plants do it all the time with beautiful results. In order to have less apprehension about your future, set clear intentions about what you want. Holding space for a favorable outcome is always a good idea. Clear quartz will hold those intentions and put your mind at ease, while umbrella plant nurtures and shelters them while they come to fruition. Working with these two elements will help you go with the flow and assume an active role in your evolution with ease.

Summer Camp

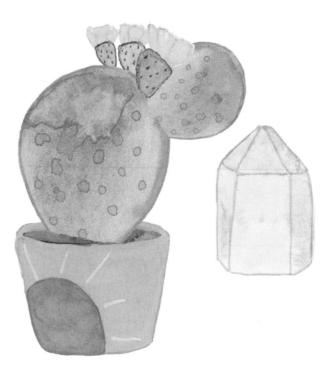

Natural, untreated topaz is sweet looking and honey-colored, but full of fiery energy from the sun. Yellow topaz is rare, but you can always find blue, white, or a toasted shade. The sun-loving stone has a mega-wattage that everyone is drawn to, its brightness motivating you to have fun and alleviating feelings of sadness. Topaz is also an ideal crystal if you want to create new friendships or strengthen existing ones.

The most extraordinary colors in the universe can be found in the desert, and some of the most alluring plants call this region their home. The climate makes everything look wild and takes your breath away. So how do you apply a desert filter to your home? Purple prickly pear cactus is a sight to behold in its natural environs, with gorgeous, watercolor pads in shades of blue-green and purple that change coloring depending on the temperature. In the spring, they produce yellow flowers, too. Smaller purple cactus, and even single pads, make excellent planter-bound houseplants, so you can have access to their warmth and vibrancy all year round.

THE VIBE

Bright and joyful summer days are some of our most treasured childhood memories. Accessing them is as simple as looking at old photos, eating your favorite warm-weather treats, or hanging out under the sun. If you were lucky, you got to go to camp. (Bonus points if you still remember every campfire song.) Camp was awesome because it was your full-time job to have fun from sunup until nightfall. If you'd like to revive this state of pure joy and play, welcome the upbeat purple prickly pear cactus and topaz into your friendship circle. A cactus that changes color depending on the weather is ready to have some fun, and its energy will put you in a summery mind-set. Golden topaz holds the warmth and vibrancy of a campfire, and will help you reconnect with your happiest memories (and create new ones). Learn to love having fun again when you work with these upbeat elements.

Super Bloom

Moss agate is basically a miniature, fossilized terrarium that you don't have to spray with water once a week. Mineral deposits that look like tiny needlepoint plants form inclusions in this gemstone, which comes in earthy tones, green and brown. It is also a horticulturalist, encouraging constant growth and renewal with its terrestrial energy. This original earth muse will instill in you a profound appreciation for nature.

Kalanchoes are easy-to-care-for miniature super blooms. The flowering succulent has neat little blossoms sprinkled among a thick swath of green leaves that resemble those of a wild strawberry plant. Wild kalanchoes grow in a variety of leaf shapes. The flowering versions you see in nurseries are not commonly found in the wild; they have been cultivated for their heirloom-like quality. These fleshy leaves efficiently store water to ensure that the dazzling spray of rosettes are long-lasting. Kalanchoes are the best that nature has to offer in terms of beauty meeting function. Few wildflowers can upstage their good looks, but it's fun to keep searching for some competition.

THE VIBE

Everything about nature is nourishing to your soul. Plants and sunlight really are the best remedies, but if you need a better reason to get outside, consider seeking out the best that your region has to offer: visit super blooms (while being conscientious of your footprint), hug a tree, rent a camper, explore hidden trails, and track down breathtaking vistas. How often do you give yourself nature breaks? Probably not often enough. There's beauty everywhere and fresh, verdant energy that you can tap into when you feel drained. And you don't have to make big plans or map out a grand adventure to get your fix. Freedom and adventure are often best experienced in smaller doses between life's busy moments. There's a place in your heart that's been longing to hook up with nature again, and moss agate will help you get there in a grounded, loving way. Likewise, flowering kalanchoes ask you to swap the indoors for the outdoors, at least once in a while. Time spent outside is good for your soul. Appreciate your houseplants and crystals at home, but make time to visit them in the wild!

ACKNOWLEDGMENTS

Thank you to my friends and family for your kind words and encouragement. To my incredible agent, Meg Thompson, thank you for your enthusiasm, guidance, and hard work. You helped me bring this dream to life. My editors, Nina Shield and Lauren Appleton, thank you for being just as excited about this book as I am, and for your patience and hard work. Laura Corless, Jess Morphew, and Lorie Pagnozzi, you made this book look amazing! Thank you to everyone at TarcherPerigee who worked on this project—you are absolute gems!

INDEX

Page numbers in *italics* indicate illustrations.

ABOUT THE AUTHOR

Tanya Lichtenstein is a writer and an illustrator with a passion for the ocean, plants, crystals, and animals. She grew up in La Jolla, California, and draws inspiration from nature. Her first book, *Cosmic Botany*, is a celebration of everything she loves.